My Ulster haven

Any similarity to real life would be strictly coincidental.

Elsa Morienval

My Ulster haven

TRANSLATED FROM FRENCH

BY STEPHANIE WATTEAU

NomBre7 éditions

"And who would have thought it thirty years before? Little Belfast could be such a beautiful city. Squatting flat in the oxter of Belfast Lough, hazily level with the water, the city was ringed with mountains and nudged by the sea. When you looked up the length of most Belfast streets, there was some kind of mountain or hill staring back at you."

Eureka street

Robert Mc Liam Wilson

13 November 2015

I'm picking up my daughter at the ice rink in Franconville. She tells me that a bomb exploded at the Stade de France. I turn on the radio and listen. It brings me right back into the atmosphere of the Northern Irish "Troubles" twenty-seven years ago!

The attacks, the hatred, the violence. How could we picture this happening here, at home, in France? No, it can’t be.

Hence, I write.

Part I

Spring 1989

I live in Épinay-sur-Seine, at my parent's house, situated in an eighteen-story building. I am 23 years old and currently finishing my first two-year University Degree (DEUG) in English at Paris XIII Villetaneuse. I'm enrolled in a Bachelor of English, and in order to do a thesis for a Master's Degree, I have to stay in an English-speaking country to improve my language skills. I had made two different applications for a French language assistant position. The role would entail assisting French teachers in a secondary school or college, primarily for classes or for small groups of pupils. The contract was around 12 hours per week.

I had taken an oral test for my first official application, this test regarded my interest in the job, my thesis topic, and general knowledge. In fact, I do not even remember the topic that I chose for the thesis. For that particular application, I had chosen three cities: Dublin, Edinburgh and Cardiff.

In the case of this application being unsuccessful, I had also made a second application which entailed the same interview process. However, this time my choices were Cork, Liverpool, and Belfast.

On that spring day, I discovered a thick envelope in the letterbox which came from Antrim, Northern Ireland. I was both happy and disappointed at the same time. In actual fact, I was deeply disappointed. I wanted to get the assistant job in Dublin, which was my first choice. I had a friend Pauline who lived in Dublin, as well as a friend Noémie, who came from my hometown in France.

I climbed up the four flights of stairs to get back home. My parents are in. I go straight to my room.

It's just not fair. I don't even open the envelope. I throw it on the ground and jump on it angrily. I am very annoyed and I don't accept that, once again, my last choice is accepted and the first one isn't. It means that my application was not good enough and that no one applies for Northern Ireland, a country at war, and a misjudged region. Who wants to go to Northern Ireland? Nobody. In fact, apart from the "Troubles", we don't know anything about Northern Ireland. We think that it must be ugly and that people are unfriendly there. That's what the people from the south say, those who live in the Republic of Ireland. Besides, their accent is really hard to understand and their English is bad. The purest English is spoken in Dublin, everyone knows that! At university, I only studied the "Troubles" and never heard of anything else other than the "Troubles", this civil war which is, by no means, a religious war but a pretext to establish a political problem. Well, that's what I got from it; because, as a matter of fact, I was not passionate about the course given by Eileen Bonvin, the senior lecturer and specialist on Northern Irish conflict. I did not understand these rivalries between the IRA and the UVF. "Bloody Sunday" comes to mind, which also evokes the U2 song. I memorised my lessons for the exams and immediately forgot them. I never understood conflicts of any kind anyway. Besides, I wasn't really meant to study English; I simply fancied speaking English in order to communicate and travel, to have my freedom. Yes, English was my passport to freedom. It opened up all borders, barriers and obstacles. It was probably naïve.

So, here I am, my job is now in Antrim, not in Dublin where

I really wanted to go.

At this point, I didn’t really care about the religious and political problems. I longed to go to Dublin. I now won’t be a French assistant there.

My parents could see that I was sad and didn’t understand. They don't even know where I applied and the reasons behind the decision. It is totally beyond them. My mother lives in her own world and has no notion of geography outside of the neighbourhood we live in.

I finally open the damn envelope. I discover a letter, from the person who would turn out to be my manager. Her name is Tiffany Richardson. Her letter is very pleasant and I love her writing: she is an Anglo-Saxon, just as I like! It is written in both English and French, which was a kind gesture. She tells me that she is happy to welcome me in Antrim, County Antrim, on the shores of Lough Neagh. What is Lough Neagh? A lake, that's for sure. Hey, there are lakes in Ulster?!

She explains that the city is one hour away, by bus or train, from Belfast and that a family will accommodate me for £20 a week, full-board. She also lets me know that I will be in charge of different groups of students in three schools: Antrim Grammar School, Antrim High School and Parkhall High School. I have to send an application back.

I lunge on a map of the British Isles that I always have on hand. Geography is a part of me. I have always been my father's co-pilot when he's driving and I love finding my way on a map. I like to know where I am and where I’m going. I see where Antrim is, and where Belfast is. I calculate the distance between Belfast and Dublin: 112 miles. I tell myself it could be worse.

I'll spend weekends in Dublin. After all, I'm leaving for Ireland, whether it's the southern one or the northern one. Never mind, I got a job in Ireland, that's a given. It's good.

My father is happy for me. My mother cries, she knows I'm going to leave the house. Leave the house for good. There would be weeks of crying and blackmailing trying to get me to change my mind.

Summer 1989

In France, we are celebrating the French Revolution bicentenary. There are shows everywhere, commemorative ceremonies. I'm going to go to Northern Ireland and I firmly believe I'll export this "free" image of France.

We are in the middle of moving from Épinay. My parents, rather my father, decided to move to Normandy, in this small fisherman's house, "Pa Pi Ja", that my mother inherited from her mother. She bears the initials of my mother and my aunts: "Pa" for Paulette, "Pi" for Pierrette and "Ja" for Janine. John my nephew, whom my parents raised after my sister passed away, just turned 14. He hangs with the wrong crowd in our neighbourhood, which has strikingly deteriorated in the space of eleven years. My father bought him a moped; he got it from my friend Zoe.

I will only be passing through Pa Pi Ja. I will be sleeping for a week in a camp bed, between the sideboard and the table, in the dining room. I'll be firstly leaving for Dublin in August, and then to Belfast. I quit my job as a cashier at Super M, a job I had for three and a half years. For the past year, I have been combining three jobs to save money and go abroad; in addition to my classes at university, where I had registered during the strikes against the Devaquet law, in 1986.

I am leaving without any regrets; I don't owe anyone anything. I feel free.

I meet up with my friend Noémie, whom I first met thanks to a French teacher a few years previous. Back then; I did not yet know that I would live in the house where she grew up. At the end of the nineties, as her mother would retire, she would offer me to live in that house; which was far cheaper than my Paris apartment.

Noémie has already lived in Dublin. There, she had met a certain Chris ; they lived together and then separated. They got back together in the summer of 1989 and finally decided to get married. I'm staying with Pauline for a couple of days. She gives me instructions and advice to protect myself from Northern Irish people! Pauline, who lives in Dundrum, south of Dublin, has been my "landlady" the previous two summers and I consider her to be my "Irish mother". I am very fond of her.

I know I will be going to Dublin as often as possible. I'm pleased; I have a place to stay there.

A newspaper headline catches my attention: "Loughlin Maginn was shot and killed by the Ulster Freedom Fighters (UFF)".

I search through my memories and remember that these Ulster Freedom Fighters are the armed wing of the Ulster Defence Association and that they are fighting against the Irish Republican Army, the armed wing of the Sinn Fein - the left-wing Republican Party - whose objective is to reunify the two Irelands in a Federal Republic. I am definitely not a historian but I hope that my stay will shed light on my poor knowledge. I'm ashamed, but never mind, that's the way it is!

That's a good start - I think. Oh Dear!

Antrim

I reach Belfast by the "Belfast express", which, at the time, takes three hours to cover the Dublin-Belfast distance. I know Tiffany will come and greet me at the bus station. The bus arrives in Newry. It is at the border between the Republic of Ireland and Northern Ireland. The bus stops. An armed soldier gets on the bus, quietly goes around and gets off. I was not expecting that. I think to myself: Where am I? What am I doing here? People are used to it, they don't even pay attention to it, it has been that way for 20 years but it has calmed down. I haven't really looked into it since my studies: how the situation has evolved or how events remain unclear to me at this time. I just know I'm here, at this moment of time.

The bus leaves and I look out over the landscape, so green, so beautiful - even on the other side of the border. Despite the sight of this soldier, I feel utterly peaceful, safe. What an odd feeling!

I arrive at the *Belfast bus station*. The station, which is in the centre of the city, behind the Europa Hotel, is under construction. Tiffany is here. She warmly welcomes me. She is a very gentle person, a little plump, reserved, with pink cheeks. Her face radiates kindness. I already know that we are going to get along. She invites me to a restaurant. A so-called French restaurant: the meal is poor quality! Tiffany apologises but, obviously, she has nothing to do with it!

She proceeds to take me to her home in Magherafelt, where I will spend the night. It is the largest city in County Derry, or Londonderry, depending on the religious beliefs (Derry for Catholics and Londonderry for Protestants). Magherafelt is located in the centre of the Ulster territory. Tiffany lives in a modest semi-detached house. The next day, she has planned to show me around her region, the Sperrin Mountains. It's beautiful, calm, despite the lack of sun. She tells me it's one of the main mountainous areas in Ireland, west of Lough Neagh. Tiffany is single, she's about ten years older than me, but she actually looks like she is twenty years older. I capture this moment with two photos: one where I've taken off my glasses - I don't want to look too nerdy. The wind is blowing in my already too voluminous hair, and I have that hilarious smile on my face revealing my forward and crooked teeth, like Laura Ingalls' in the eternal series "The little house on the prairie". And this genuinely amuses me. The second one shows Tiffany, in that same wind, wearing a colourless raincoat. In the background, stand these magnificent green mountains that can only be seen from this place.

At the end of the day, she takes me to Paddy's, her colleague and friend. She is head of the French department of one of the schools where I will be teaching. Paddy lives in "the Hermitage". It is a large estate, a kind of small mansion like the ones you see in English soap operas. It's big. It's beautiful. This is a totally new and uncharted environment to me. Paddy is the opposite of Tiffany: outgoing, tall, lean, with unfailing confidence. She and her husband are very wealthy; they are part of a well-known family in Northern Ireland, the Johnstons. There is a very jovial atmosphere. They are lovely people. When

Paddy speaks English to me, she is articulating as much as possible. I’m spending a night at their home before going to my host family in Antrim the next day.

She shows me to my room and I just stand there, taken aback. It’s a castle room! I don't even dare put down my travel bag, as I feel so ordinary in this royal setting. I don’t dare to settle down. I go back down to their huge kitchen and chat to the very joyful Paddy.

The next morning, Paddy takes me to the Mc Kendrys’, the family who is hosting me during this school year. It’s Friday, classes don’t start until Monday.

Kathleen greets me. She is a very welcoming, smiley woman, who looks motherly. She is also warm. She shows me to my room. This is unexpected. A real bedroom, overlooking their garden. A very green garden, like the rest of the landscape. I feel like I'm dreaming. It is "cozy" and comfortable. I know I'm going to feel at home here!

I drop my luggage off and join Kathleen in the kitchen. She shows me around the house. It’s fairly big. A home in a housing estate. A kitchen-living room, a dining room and the "TV room" which allows them to entertain guests before going to the dining room.

Kathleen immediately offers me a cup of tea in the TV room. We chat and I learn that she is a childcare assistant in a nursery. She works next door to Parkhall High School, one of the schools where I am going to work as an assistant. The family has four children. The eldest is my age, the second a year younger, she is a nurse. The third is 14 years old and the last one is 9 years old.

The previous year they had housed the French assistant, Anne-Marie, whom I would meet during the year, as she would spend a few days at the Mc Kendrys' with her sister.

I meet Eamon, Kathleen's husband. He is a rather short, kind of Spanish-looking, dark-haired man, who is very agile with an incomprehensible, yet pleasant accent. He's always in top form, always in a good mood. He listens to Irish folk music; the family is Catholic, therefore faithful to the Catholic traditions of the Republic of Ireland. I will see the divide throughout my stay, a divide that you only find here in Ulster.

Kathleen says to me: "Tea is ready" which means to me that the tea is ready, literally! I just had a cup; it's 5:30 p.m. I am expected in the dining room. I then understand that "Tea" also means "meal" since we drink tea at the table and not water, like we do in France!

I really like this place. I'm dreaming of projects that are full of hope and, yes, that will come true. I'm learning to live on Northern Irish time, with its difficulties, its peculiar accent, and its eating habits - hated by the inhabitants of the Republic. I'm trying to adjust to the pronunciation, which I find "distorted" but funny.

The weekend is coming. Everyone wakes up when they feel like it. Times are very flexible, "Tea" can be at any time of the day like 2 p.m., 3 p.m., or even 4 p.m., but there is only one. Apart from this "Tea" we only eat toast or a large ice cream in the middle of the day. I've had numerous hypoglycaemia linked to this change of rhythm; since I came from a family where scheduling is rigorous, meals are at set times, and nonnegotiable.

The weather is nice and mild. The Mc Kendrys decide to take me to visit the Glens in County Antrim. Both come from a valley in the Glens. I will also later learn that the Armada stayed in these Glens, hence the Spanish type of certain inhabitants in Northern Ireland. Twenty-four Armada ships, diverted from their destination by storms, were wrecked, from the coast of Antrim to north Kerry, in September 1588.

The couple seem genuinely happy in life. They tease each other all the time and they love each other. They show me a great deal of affection. I have never been given so much consideration. I am however only a tenant.

We are hiking; it's very pleasant. I'm taking lots of photos. The scenery is both magical and wild, it's like a dream. I quickly realise the potential of this stay.

During this time, no one talks to me about the "Troubles". It's like they didn't exist.

***

Monday is the first day of school. Kathleen - who asks me to imperatively call her "Kate" in the street, and not Kathleen - shows me the way to the school where I am going to work. Kathleen is the "Gaelic", therefore Catholic, name for Kathrin. Kathreen, or Kate, is neutral. Families are listed as "Catholic" or "Protestant". It makes the secular French woman that I am laugh; but soon, it won't be something to laugh about.

I am due to arrive at 9 a.m. at Parkhall High School. Paddy and Tiffany greet me. They show me the administrative premises, and the school that I find both luxurious and gigantic. They also introduce me to the Principal, a tall redhead with a hoarse voice. He is very welcoming. It's the morning assembly time. Assemblies are an opportunity to get children to discuss and think about current issues. The assemblies also aim to provide information on school life, to highlight the work carried out in the different classes, and to give students the many individual awards that exist in the English system (certificates of achievement, stars of the week, academic awards, etc.). These "gatherings" are religious in the sense that speeches and prayers refer to God but no specific denomination is mentioned, neither Catholic nor Protestant, the only two religions present in Northern Ireland. I am quite uncomfortable. I have the impression of being at mass; still, I find this kind of funny because I do not know enough about the school system.

After receiving my schedule, I meet the students in their class. The level of French is very poor. But French is a difficult language of Latin origin. English is an oral language that we learn "globally". In this establishment, I will only have Secondary School students. At break time, I am introduced to the teachers.

In the afternoon, I introduce myself at the Grammar School. An even more luxurious school. In fact, "Grammar schools" recruit only the best students via an exam-based entry process. "High schools" are "comprehensive schools" which educate all students, whatever their level.

I ask for my manager, Mr Wilson, head of the French department. He shows up very quickly. He is about fifty, very upright, very self-confident, with blue eyes, and a slightly receding hairline. His French is perfect, almost without any accent. I notice a somewhat unhealthy gaze from him, I don't know why. He informs me that I am going to teach small groups of 6th Formers and Upper 6th Form students, in oral work. I would later have very fond memories of these students.

A few weeks later, I started a French club in the school. It was called the "Kermitterand club" in reference to the presentation of the French program "le bebête show" (the crazy beast show), pretty popular back then. One of my students, very gifted in drawing, made a poster for the French club with this frog which elicited a lot of comments but which represented France so well! The most famous frog in France: our President of the Republic, François Mitterand! A journalist from the Antrim gazette even came to interview me in my office at the French club. It was the first time that a language assistant has created anything in addition to her twelve-hour work contract! I don't need to go to the students, I don't even have to ask: they come to me and try to speak French, poorly most of the time.

The third establishment is another "high school", I work only one hour a week at this school. I can't remember a lot about my time there. The level of French is appalling, including that of the only French teacher. However, she is kind and would invite me to dinner twice. The students are very badly behaved and are not interested in French. I started a "croissant, chocolate croissant and apple turnover" project to win them over. Serial baking all these pastries will prove pretty successful.

***

I am discovering the centre of Antrim, a fairly small commuter town; I perceive this more and more everyday. It has no character except for its train station and the "Marina", the small harbour on the lake, Lough Neagh. It's a long distance to walk and I will only go twice during my stay. As in all commuter towns, there is a large shopping centre. I will take a wee daily stroll there and often meet my students with their parents who will always greet me with a grateful smile. The newspaper article went around town and the kids must have hurried to say they knew me. I am, in fact, a sort of curiosity. I am "the French lady".

What impresses me the most about this town, and I will see this in other towns as well, is the police station. Its size is disproportionate. It is a huge and large building, solidly constructed, surrounded by a high double fence, overhung with barbed wire. I have never seen this in my life. When I take a less travelled path, I hear small cameras turning in my direction. It amuses me and I sometimes even make faces at them. All towns are under close surveillance.

***

At the end of my first week, I take the bus to Belfast. One hour. One hour of a deserted road, no houses, no villages. The scenery of hills and fields unfolds at my window. Coming from the city, I am completely disoriented, dumbfounded, seized by this unusual landscape. This green transports me to my deepest inner peace. I will go every week as I enjoy it so much.

Belfast is the capital of Northern Ireland, but it is a tiny city in County Antrim. Mountains surround it, well, let's say hills, and in winter their peaks are covered with snow. It is fabulous. It is difficult to describe Belfast without talking about the barriers at each street entrance. Armed soldiers, however quiet they may be, are very present. Huge police stations in every neighbourhood. The city is strategically under control. I'm expecting an old city centre like in Dublin but can't find it because there isn't one. The city centre is new. It is even constantly under reconstruction because of the attacks. The Luft

Waffe already demolished it during World War II. Nevertheless, I find the stores that I like, I'm exploring. Clothes are cheap and so is food. I'm finding French products that I will start to miss after a few weeks and that I will be happy to share with my hosts. Brie, Camembert, olives etc. I can only find these products at M&S or in delicatessens, but I enjoy searching the streets and stores. There is at least one bomb threat every time I go downtown to department stores.

Only the City Hall and Ulster Hall, where I will later have the pleasure of singing, are original buildings. I will not go until much later in the west of the city because of the wall that separates the two districts - That of the Catholics and that of the Protestants. It's almost like a small Berlin. The district of Falls road, the street that crosses the west of the city, is Catholic. While Protestants, pro-British Loyalists, live in the district of Shankill road, the street that crosses the east. These are two worlds that do not know each other, and that never meet except with the intention of attacking the enemy. Lynching outside establishments is common. Hatred is present on both sides. And, even though I've never looked into this, I'm learning it anyway.

Sometimes, I'll take the train to Belfast. The route is not as pleasant but the line serves other areas where I like to walk. I like the Botanical Gardens area, which is very close to Queen's University. It is the students' district where you can easily find coffee shops and cafes at low prices. Queen's University - formerly Queen's College, Belfast - was one of four universities built in Ireland by the British Crown when the island was entirely ruled by Britain. This was long before the island was partitioned in 1921 between the independent Southern Ireland (today's Republic of Ireland) and Ulster in the north.

In Belfast I will also visit the docks. It is a creepy, abandoned place, where the flea market sits. This district, where the largest port in Europe was located, saw the famous Titanic being built before it tragically sank in 1912. This part of the industrial and working class Belfast, dating from the Victorian era, will be completely transformed after the Good Friday Agreement in 1998, and will once again become a lively and culturally rich neighbourhood. There, the Titanic museum will find its place. The docks will be improved.

In previous years, bombings were daily events, the police and army would only drive around in armoured vehicles, Protestant militias blindly killed innocent Catholics, and the IRA itself conducted a terribly harsh and violent campaign as well. Thankfully, this is now part of the past.

***

I learn in the media that Margaret Thatcher will be visiting in September to congratulate the members of the UDR - Ulster Defence Regiment - for their bravery. But I remain quite detached from the news, and yet...

One day, while happily having tea at KFC, I'm the victim of an attack. I cannot believe it. Be that as it may, a young man is in a car near the KFC entrance, ready to throw a grenade. Two armed men tell us to lie down on the ground. People are screaming in fear. With someone else, we cover people lying on the ground with a chair. I don't even think about it. I am not afraid. Death does not scare me. What a strange feeling. I don't remember how long this moment lasted. Maybe fifteen, twenty minutes? But the police arrive and neutralise this 17-year-old man, a young fanatic, and his two friends.

We got lucky: Either he didn't have the guts to throw his grenade, or it didn't work.

I leave the KFC, the police still present. I'm headed for the bus station. I'm at least an hour and a half late and I can't warn the Mc Kendrys. I know they will worry, as I am always very punctual. The time spent at KFC must have been longer than I thought.

I get on the bus and start shaking like a leaf. I suddenly realise what just happened. I can't wait to get back to Antrim.

I arrive at the Mc Kendrys', who are waiting for me for "Tea". I tell them everything. They are sorry and ashamed. Ashamed of their country. The eldest son even comes to discuss with me, he is sorry about this "bad bother" as he says.

I'm finally realising that I live in Northern Ireland with this aspect that I may have overlooked until now, and that I am living this from the inside now.

***

After a few weeks, I enrol in a German evening course at the Antrim Forum, the leisure centre. As I register, management asks me if I can give French lessons, for the Forum, to adults. This offer is a pleasant surprise and I immediately agree but inform them that I have to take exams in Paris and will be away for a week. They tell me that they will wait for me because there are no other French people in Antrim.

During this German course, I meet a young man, very interested in French and who comes to talk to me. His name is Mark. He is very respectful, quite small, blond with blue eyes, and a cartoon character face. A very expressive face. Basically, "a funny face". He is witty and breathes life. He has a car and can drive me around. From then on, all my trips in Northern Ireland will depend on his availability. His kindness and helpfulness surprise me. He is unemployed, like 18% of the population in Northern Ireland, but has a "public utility" job at Parkhall High School in order to get 10% more benefits. He never liked school but is interested in everything; he has a fairly extensive culture. He comes from the working class. His father was often absent and I think he must have been in charge from a very young age. At Parkhall, a Spanish assistant shows up in October, her name is Aurora. We will become friends and still are. Mark suggests outings in pubs, or in certain districts of Belfast to see monuments that are inaccessible by transport, with his old car which often breaks down, doesn't even have a radiator, and which he repairs himself! We regularly offer to pay for petrol but he refuses, so we buy him drinks. Unlike his friends, he does not drink alcohol.

He has a girlfriend: Evlyn. She's lovely. They will eventually split up and, even though I'm longing for it, I will not replace her in his heart. What a pity!

***

With Aurora - who is a young woman my age, she has very dark hair, she's plump, she moves pretty slowly but is extremely sociable - we visit a few cities. She will even come with me to visit my friend Noémie in the south of Dublin, in Bray. She will end up moving to Belfast as she is assigned to two schools very far apart and because she loves the city. Antrim is too quiet for her.

My landlords are such gems. I appreciate them a little more

every day. Once, I remember returning home very late, or rather in the wee hours, at the Mc Kendrys' and I had forgotten my key. I was clueless. I stayed behind the door forever! I ended up ringing the bell. I was afraid I'd get grounded, like a little girl who did something she shouldn't have done. I must have been pretty pale. But then, Kathleen opens the door, her eyes full of sleep, and just smiles. I deeply apologise for forgetting my key, for waking her up in the middle of the night. She asks me if I had a good evening, she is actually happy for me! I am amazed. Not only does she not reprimand me but she is even glad for me. I had fun and that is the most important thing. I have never experienced this before. I feel loved.

***

I'm going back to Paris to take two mid-term exams for my two-year University Degree (DEUG); I will only pass one out of two. But I do have to get this Degree.

My friends Nathalie and Valérie, who are hosting me in Paris, give me an incredible surprise: they take me to see Francis Huster, at the theatre, in Camus' "The Stranger". At the time, I was a great fan of Francis Huster. At the end of the show, I go and see him and imagine that he is going to be obnoxious and pedantic. To my surprise, he is very genuine. He even asks me personal questions! I tell him that I'm a teacher in Northern Ireland and I would love my students to know a little bit about him. He gives me several posters and dedicates one for the Antrim students. He even asks me which wording I wish to teach them! I was not expecting that. I find this actor very kind and much nicer than I had imagined!

I was eager to get back to Belfast.

My friend Nathalie tells me that she will come by and visit me in Antrim in the spring.

When I come home, the Mc Kendrys are waiting for me. They ask me if I passed my exams.

My parents don't know that I came back to France for a week. I was careful not to tell them. Otherwise, it would have been all about blackmailing and a blame game. Especially from my mother.

As I am going to the Forum to take my position as a French teacher for adults, I am told - to my greatest disappointment - that a French woman filled it. I am full of anger. "There are no French people in Antrim", I have heard this often enough!

A few days later, a student from Parkhall comes to see me and speaks French to me. Her name is Corinne. She tells me that her mother is French and does replacements in the establishment, when there are needs. She is present that day and I meet her in the teachers' room. She comes to greet me very kindly and introduces herself, Catherine. She is a fairly tall, well-grounded woman, with blue eyes, and short, wavy hair. She has an outspokenness that I truly like. She tells me that she is happy: she found a job at the Forum. I answer to her: "oh, so you're the one who took my job!"

We became very close friends during my stay in Ulster. Our relationship has been of the utmost importance during all this time.

Catherine is so happy to meet a French woman in Antrim that she immediately invites me to her home. I tell Kathleen about it and she tells me that she knows her because she and her husband had opened a frozen food store in the 1980s but it had not worked out.

Catherine and her family live in a rent-controlled housing in the heights of Antrim, not far from Mark's. In the street, the smell of turf is coming out from the chimneys. Social housing in Antrim is nothing like ours in the Paris suburbs. Tenants have a house with a front garden and a back garden. A kitchen, a utility room, a living room and upstairs bedrooms, these are "garden-cities". People don't live on top of each other. There is space; there are so few inhabitants in Northern Ireland!

Catherine is married to Padraic Hughes (namesake of an IRA terrorist!) and has three children: Corinne, 11, Chiaran, 8, and Niall, 3. She came to Northern Ireland in the 1970s, of her own free will, as a language assistant. The Northern Irish conflicts were the subject of her thesis for her English Master's Degree at the Nanterre University. She met Padraic, of Catholic origin but atheist, and she stayed in Northern Ireland. Next, they went to live in France, in Paris, where Corinne was born. Padraic ran a grocery store and Catherine gave English lessons. Padraic's brother offered to open a frozen food store in Antrim and so they moved back to Northern Ireland. The business only lasted two years; the frozen goods market was not yet customary. They also played classical music which did not please customers. But above all, I imagine that they were probably too idealistic to be business minded.

When I meet them, Padraic is unemployed, like many. He does some odd illegal job here and there, as a greyhound race bookie for example. Catherine does replacements in Antrim's schools, classroom supervisions, and tries to give French lessons to adults.

After all, I am really very happy that she was able to get this job, she needs it much more than I do, on my own.

Despite the financial problems, there is a lot of joy in their home. It's full of life. I am regularly invited to eat. Catherine is clearly happy to have a French woman with whom she can interact. I'm somewhat embarrassed because of all the attention she gives me. We talk about everything: family, culture, politics, and linguistics. The Northern Irish way of life. It is very fulfilling.

It was Catherine who explained to me her first three years, a "grace period", in Ulster. She arrived in the early 1970s, easily renewing her contract, as a French assistant, twice during the "Bloody Sunday" times; indeed, there were not many requests! On January 30, 1972, when the British Military attacked civilians in a peaceful protest, it killed fourteen people in Derry, in the Bogside district. The end of the 60s had seen the situation deteriorate, but the 70s were the bloodiest.

As planned, I go to Dublin as often as I can. I am staying with Noémie in Bray. She and Chris are planning their wedding. I go with her to wedding dress shops for her fittings. It's fun. I'm taking pictures of her. She is stunning.

Noémie works at the "Alliance Française" in Dublin. Alliance teachers often go out together and I join them, just like if I were one of them. It's pleasant but very intellectual. It feels strange to see so many French people gathered in Dublin. I still love Dublin very much, but I almost prefer the calm that reigns in Antrim and not being surrounded by too many French people. How can I speak of calm when the attacks divide the people of this country? Yet, my body is pure bliss, calm and serene.

I absolutely do not regret coming to Northern Ireland.

Granny !

One evening at the Mc Kendrys, the phone rings. Kathleen calls me; it is for me.

I hear my mother's not so clear voice. She has had a few drinks, but she is conscious enough to tell me: "These are crucial times. Your grandmother is finally dead".

She announces this to me, from her point of view, joyful news. My paternal grandmother, Valentine, her rival, has closed her eyes for good.

I will not go to the funeral, timing is too short and I just took time off for my exams.

My sister writes me a letter. The only one I have ever received from her. I will not receive any more in the future. She shares her grief with me. She is sad. I remain shocked at the way my mother broke the news to me. This is not the first time that she has acted this way.

I feel so at home at the Mc Kendry's.

***

At the beginning of December, I get sick. The flu is rife and is not as well treated in Northern Ireland as it is in France. I hear on TV that a lot of people are dying from it every week.

As my back is very painful, I go to see the doctor. I have my "medical card" and I do not pay the doctor, everything is taken care of. Doctors are all grouped in a large medical centre; this does not yet exist in France. Each patient has an appointment every five minutes.

I end up in an office where the doctor asks me to sit down. I explain to him that my back hurts and he tells me that he is going to examine me. As the French woman that I am, I get undressed, but the doctor seems shocked and suggests that I put my clothes back on! He places the stethoscope on two layers of clothing. I'm guessing he can't hear anything. He doesn't really examine me more than that. He only has five minutes per patient. He writes me a prescription for paracetamol and cough syrup even though I am not coughing.

I stop by the pharmacy at the back of a large cosmetic centre and get the drugs. I don't pay. I go back to the Mc Kendrys', aching all over. I take paracetamol and just go to bed.

At noon, Kathleen, who never comes home at this hour, purposely returns to check on me and take care of me, if necessary. How is that even possible? I am not her daughter and she is worried about me. My being sick doesn't bother Kathleen and she doesn't blame me for it. She asks me if I want tea or soup, or if I need anything else. I don't know how to thank her. This brings tears to my eyes.

She very quickly goes back to the nursery.

Since living with the Mc Kendrys, I'm allowed to shower every day and to wash my clothes whenever I want. I have never experienced this before. At my parents' house, I could only shower and wash my clothes once a week because water is precious and expensive and, also, it wears out the clothes and the skin. I can also use all kinds of towels or bath sheets. This is all new to me.

In Irish homes, bathrooms are full of cosmetics. In our home, one single bar of soap thrones on its soap dish and one shampoo, the least expensive possible, stands on the edge of the bathtub. That same bathtub, which is only used by John, my nephew, because he is young; hence, he has the right to do so. A bathtub is for children only, not for adults.

I have to stop working for a week because of this flu that is beating me down. I resume a few days before leaving for France at the end of December. A teacher proudly asks me to teach the Christmas carol "Il est né le divin enfant" (He is born, the Divine child) to her students. She thinks I will be moved or touched, I can feel it, because it's a typical French Christmas religious song, but instead I'm uncomfortable again as I don't know the lyrics, I've never learned them. We do not sing this kind of song in my family or actually, we do, but a rearranged version. Granny's companion had taught me this version: "The divine child was born, turn around and we will blow the horn". I ask this teacher for a day or two, as I need to review the lyrics. Of course, she accepts. Phew! I ask her if she has the text, as I'm not sure I can I find it here, in Northern Ireland. So I am finally learning for the first time the true version of "Il est né le divin enfant". We sing it with the children, the next day. It all goes very well and the teacher is delighted. She merrily thanks me.

Little by little, I realise that I lack a religious instruction. That will later play tricks on me during text studies.

***

It's been several weeks now since I started singing in the Antrim choir with little or no musical education. I learn to know sacred music, requiems. The choirmaster is proud to have a Frenchwoman in his choir and I, myself, am discovering that I'm enjoying it.

Before leaving for France, I cook a French meal for my hosts: turkey cutlets marinated in white wine and olive oil with a creamy sauce, pan-fried fresh mushrooms and sautéed potatoes. They have a notable respect for what I prepared and assist me in serving the ones sitting closest to me at the table.

Once everyone is served, I see Eamon taking the HP sauce, which always sits on the table during meals, as well as the ketchup. He pours a good squirt of HP over his cutlet already covered with cream sauce and that is when I cannot help but gasp and squeal, while calming myself down! He looks at me and understands that he did something he shouldn't have. I gently smile and explain to him that in France (at that time anyway!) when we already have sauce that is part of the recipe, we do not need to add another sauce as we would here. He apologises and I tell him that his reaction is normal, that he cannot know the French eating habits.

I am anxious about going to my parents' place, Pa Pi Ja. I will only stay there for three days, outside of Christmas. I don't want to spend a single Christmas with them anymore. It is over.

I go between my friends' welcoming homes.

I spend an evening at my sister and brother-in-law's who ask me if I finally have a "man" in my life.

I flee.

I take advantage of this stay in France to buy a dictionary of symbols to explain the bean ("la fève", now a china figurine) in the cake - a galette with frangipane, and Kings' day in France. I buy a bunch of small gifts for my hosts, for Catherine and her family, and for my students. I refine my knowledge of the French and French-speaking world.

I am so delighted to be leaving again for this peace haven where, attacks and tanks are all over. What a contradiction!

When I go back to Ireland, I actually go home.

***

Catherine invites me over as soon as I arrive, in early January. She tells me that they finally have a spot in the hospital so that their last child, Niall, can have his tonsils and adenoids surgically removed. They made the request eighteen months ago. The medical system is really flawed in Northern Ireland. I feel like I'm in the Middle Ages or at least going back fifty years, as France was back then. A pharmacist friend sends me medicines on demand; she inserts them in thick magazines in an envelope, as it is forbidden to send them abroad.

I invite my girl friends who will soon come. First my friend Nathalie's niece; she is 15 years old and wants to improve her English. We will be visiting a number of sites with Mark, when he is available, and Aurora. It is pure bliss, I introduce her to where I'm living as if I had always lived there and I am so proud of it. Landscapes unfold before me, one after the other, with a depth that I will never find elsewhere - except perhaps in certain landscapes of Quebec that I'll visit 15 years later or in Normandy, in "little Ireland", in Cotentin.

Then it's Nathalie who comes during the Easter holiday. As I am invited to Noémie's wedding in Bray, in the south of Dublin, she comes along. This allows her to visit the north a bit and then Dublin. Nathalie does not recognise me, she finds me fulfilled and relaxed.

I'm living my life. My real life, a life I have never experienced before, with so much intensity and authenticity on my part. I don't encounter hostility and yet the region is at war. I don't understand this. I don't understand these religious cleavages, for me it doesn't make sense.

This life, however, fills my heart and soul with peace and serenity.

Overall, I have a good connection with students. The ones with whom I have the most memories are those I am prepping for the French oral exam, the lower and upper 6ths. I have to make them converse on imposed themes such as drugs, the massacre of baby seals, marriage, etc. I use the texts they were given and add pop rock songs by French artists like Jean-Jacques Goldman or Telephone as well as newspaper articles. That is how I taught them Goldman's song "Elle a fait un bébé toute seule" (She had a baby on her own). The students love the American beat of the song but as they start understanding the lyrics I can see they are shocked, especially when the singer says: "puis son gamin, c'est presque le mien, sauf qu'il a les yeux bleus" (and her kid, he is almost mine, except that he has blue eyes). I can feel that I am going too far and yet, single-parent families exist in France and Ireland, but here these words are immoral. Following my teaching of this song, I have a discussion with teachers who make me understand that we shouldn't be "perverting" young people! I talk to them about philosophy and ask them why there is no philosophy course in schools. I am told that these students are too stupid to understand philosophy. I start to protest and argue that no one is stupid and that it's all about education. I quickly understand that I shouldn't insist. I realise that I am French and that education and schooling are very different outside my country. In fact, I find this entertaining and often provoke the teachers who do not have the freedom of thought that we have in France.

Some times spent with the students are difficult to narrate because they happened while we spoke. Here is one that I will try to recount. One day, one of my students comes to me at the end of a session and says: "Miss, murwd!!!" I immediately understand what he is trying to say but I pretend not to understand what he means. Therefore, I ask him to repeat himself. After three times, I tell him that I feel like I'm hearing a cow mooing. I tell him that if he wants to decently insult a French, he better pronounce it correctly. Otherwise, he will be the laughing stock and will look ridiculous. The pupil feels a little "stupid"! I teach him to pronounce the five letters correctly by telling him that it is the same sound as "t'aime" (love you) in "je t'aime" (I love you). And I also make him pronounce the word "fair". Wanting to insult me, it turns out he had a beautiful lesson in phonetics. After this rather fun episode, he would always come to say goodbye at the end of each session.

What I cannot forget are these answers to the usual questions:

"What did you do this weekend? Or what did you do during the holidays?" I would get:

- “jay lavay la vwatour dugh mon purr” (I washed my father’s car)

- “jay vowyajay sir l’avion” (I travelled on the plane)

- “jay vowyajay sir le train” (I travelled on the train)

- “juh swee allay a la lesh-vitreen (I went window shopping!)

There is no better way to learn the English language structure than by teaching a foreign language in an English speaking country!

These “Frenglish” phrases still echo in my head as if it were yesterday. Pure joy!

And I always answer with irony that if they literally travel "on" (*sur*) the plane, in French, they will be very cold or they will die! Same thing with "on" the train! I'm having fun.

***

Throughout this school year, the heads of the French departments and teachers invite me to their homes and take me out.

This is how I am invited to Mr Wilson's, of Antrim Grammar School. Of all the teachers, he is the one who stands out the most for his perfect French. He even asks me grammar questions that

I cannot answer but which I then elucidate very quickly. It's a game, a challenge between us.

So I get to his place on a Sunday afternoon. He lives in a fairly decent part of Antrim, on a street lined with large houses. When the door opens, I discover a dark and austere universe. His wife, who seems submissive, made French toast for "tea". The furniture is old-fashioned and the armchairs are old and threadbare. Everything is tidy, organised.

Mr Wilson gets royal treatment from his wife, a woman of few words. He asks me what my religion is. I tell him that I am a baptised Catholic but that I have not received any religious teaching and that I do not practice. I am an atheist.

He tells me he's a Baptist. I don't know Baptists. I quickly realise that this religion is sectarian. Mr Wilson is very bossy. The family took a vow of poverty but, from his status as head of department, I know that he earns a good living and that they are not poor. He suggests that I come and meet them at church, their church. As I am curious, I am tempted. I will go once but will come out very quickly ; feeling like this is not right and unhealthy.

Later on, Tiffany, my manager - my "boss" as I call her - takes me to visit the "American Folk Park" in Omagh, in the Sperrins region. It's an open-air museum, a reconstructed village. Two million people leaving for the United States, recounting three centuries of Northern Irish emigration in the 18th and 19th centuries. This park highlights the economic difference between the two denominations, the lower social status of Catholic families in particular. I am very interested in this museum of colossal historical wealth showing the great poverty of some and the social rise of others, arriving in the new world. The reconstruction of the Pennsylvanian village, where immigrants arrived, makes me think of "The little house on the prairie"!

The city of Omagh will unfortunately be the scene of a particularly deadly attack (29 dead and 220 wounded) on August 15, 1998, perpetrated by a dissident group of the IRA, in opposition to the peace agreement, signed four months earlier.

In turn, Paddy takes me to lunch in a magnificent, yet very sober restaurant overlooking a cliff by the sea. I eat salmon in "steak" for the first time. I find it delicious. I also relish the breath-taking view of the green hills abundantly watered by the rain in front of us. So much peace and inner joy flow through me!

***

The people in charge of the language assistants gather us in Ballymena in the north of Antrim. This moment is very convivial, they organised role-plays for us. Some counsellors need our help to do skits that the students will listen to; this motivates the assistants. A counsellor who is seconded to Northern Ireland, but is part of the London education board, individually asks us if we wish to renew a year of assistantship in Northern Ireland. If this is the case, she provides us with a letter of recommendation for the following year. I immediately apply. I also ask for an application at the University of Villetaneuse to renew my assignment. I will receive a positive response in June.

I meet Florence and Dominique, whom I will meet again the following year. With Florence, we go on hikes when the weather is nice. We will hike the Mourne Mountains in May and get sunstroke! Our Irish hosts and friends won't believe us: getting sunstroke in Ireland is impossible! We will also visit Rathlin Island, an island now turned into a bird sanctuary. We will stay with a former African colonist who transformed part of his house into a youth hostel. An alcoholic woman will show us around part of the north coast. How reckless! But I'm sure Florence still thinks about this. After all, it's a good memory.

***

I didn't know about the Giant's Causeway before going to the north of Ireland. Apart from Connemara known thanks to Michel Sardou's song “Les lacs du Connemara” (Connemara’s Loughs) or Galway through "Le taxi mauve" (The mauve taxi) by Michel Déon, I have never heard of the Giant's Causeway. That year, I went there three times. I discovered a gem that I didn't know existed. I still wonder why the south of Ireland is more often valued than the north? I find that unfair.

From a distance, the Giant's Causeway looks like a large volcanic organ. It is grandiose, unusual, and “inhuman". If I say "inhuman", it is because I consider that humans could not have imagined a more beautiful masterpiece. It is a natural wonder made of basalt. A volcano that froze as it rose.

Legend has it that this place was built by the giant Finn McCool in order to allow his Scottish rival to come and challenge him in single combat. Another legend says that when the Scottish giant arrived in Ireland, his opponent had turned himself into a baby. Seeing his size, he imagined his father's stature, got scared and ran back, destroying part of the Causeway. It was not until the 19th Century that the origin of this gigantic paving, dating back more than 40 million years, was discovered!

Over the months, I step into the legends, into the fantasy Ireland carries when I have always resisted the "stories" I was told in school or that my mother tried to make me believe. For me, it didn't make sense and I just found them stupid because I knew they weren't genuine. I only know how to live in realism, I leave no room to my imagination because I need to master everything in my daily life. Here, the decor is itself so legendary, I can find meaning in these "stories", a certain authenticity. They belong to the country and its inhabitants.

I'm starting to let my imagination wander.

By the end of the school year, I'm writing poems.

***

With Parkhall High School, Tiffany, Paddy and I go to a mini camp in a specialised institution. The goal is to "educate" the students, to introduce them to French in a cultural and fun way. Parkhall is an establishment that welcomes a majority of students coming from disadvantaged families. This is an important project for Parkhall and the French teachers organise the activities. I am, of course, invited to actively participate, which I happily do. Paddy asks me to come to her place and help her cook a "bourguignon" and a "ratatouille". It's a real pleasure. Her kitchen is so vast and so well equipped that it is easy to cook without getting in each other's way.

The camp lasts two days and takes place in Ballycastle, a town on the north coast, not far from the Giant's Causeway. It's pouring rain during both days. The activities are dense and the students do not appreciate the dishes we prepared for them. For me, it is a failure. Once back, I talk to the school principle and tell him that it could have been "better". So, he asks me what was not ok. I share with him my feeling that the students have not learned anything and that they did not care about French, or French culture. He tells me that we can never do better but that we are doing "well" and that it is already not that bad! I will experience that same feeling eight years later in the north of Paris with students from underprivileged backgrounds.

I remember taking a walk with Tiffany in the Ballycastle harbour to take a break during this mini camp; under grey skies and pouring rain the wind was so strong you couldn't hear yourself talking but it was funny and we just laughed about it.

***

In June, I have to leave and wait for the university's positive answer for a second year in Northern Ireland. I know that the opinion is favourable and that, given the low number of applications, I have a good chance of going back but I still don’t yet know. I am preoccupied and sad.

I leave the Mc Kendrys with a very heavy heart - and I choose my words carefully here. Kathleen cries too, hugs me, reassures me, and tells me that I will be back in two months.

Eamon takes me to the airport and cries too.

Valérie comes to pick me up at the Charles de Gaulle Airport. I see my girl friends in Paris and leave for Normandy. I am apprehensive. I am worried.

Pa Pi Ja, July 1990

My father comes to pick me up at the Coutances train station. He is, of course, very happy to see me. We are driving towards Regnéville sur mer. They have been living in this little house for a year now. I don't know what shape I'm going to find my mother in. I almost want to turn around, but here I am.

We arrive at Pa Pi Ja. As I'm entering the house, she comes out of the kitchen. She probably just hid her glass of wine somewhere, in a corner, or in a cupboard. As usual, she's staggering, her hair is not done, and she's poorly dressed. Her glasses are dirty. As I get closer to her, I'm holding my breath, and I kiss her without any tenderness, I cannot. She doesn't ask me how I'm doing and I don't ask her anything either. We are having lunch. My father is the one who moves around. My mother wanders between the kitchen and the living room, without sitting down. She eats very little at the table because she is already full of liquids. She is never hungry. John asks me questions, he's happy to see me too. I know he will leave the table as soon as we finish eating; he is fifteen.

When the meal is over, my mother begins to vociferate, blaming me for my absence, insulting me until she ends up calling me a "bitch". John grabs something off the table and throws it in her face. My father says nothing. He remains passive as always.

I'm not even talking to my mother, I simply go and get my travel bag - it's not even open yet - and ask my father to take me to my cousin Paul's.

I don't want to be insulted for no reason anymore. It is absolutely unbearable.

My father complies, my mother keeps shouting and calling me a "bitch".

We get into the car, my father says to me: "You know your mother, yet, you are leaving?" and I answer: “Yes, precisely, I know her and that is why I am leaving, I know her too well! Daddy, I've only been home for two hours and she’s calling me a bitch, do you find that normal?”

My father is speechless; he doesn't recognise me. I've never rebelled, until today.

He drops me off at Paul's, who doesn't know I'm coming, but he had offered to host me, just in case!

My father will try to call me. As I need a car and Paul is a mechanic, my father offers me a second-hand car, an old Ami 8, for 500 Francs (£70). He tells me that he argued with my mother over what she told me and that he wants me to come back. I find a job as a cashier at the supermarket in Coutances, but quit after three weeks because I was offered another job at Cetelem, in Neuilly, for the month of August. I don't give in. I eventually accept an invitation to lunch but, then again, as I arrive at Pa Pi Ja, my mother says to me: "I hear that now you are pumping fuel at Paul's garage?" I do not answer but the insults resume, I jump in my car and leave again. I will only come back once before leaving for Paris, just to say goodbye to them. Then I will hardly give them any news for months. I won't be able to anymore.

During those three weeks, Paul takes advantage of my vulnerability and asks me for money, but that's another story!

At the end of July, I finally receive my assignment for a new assistant position: I will be in Belfast at Wellington College, a very large establishment. It comforts me to know I will be leaving soon.

In August, I am staying at my sister and brother-in-law's. I am doing them a favour as they are going on holidays and I can watch their house and feed their cat. I work in the mail department; it's an assembly line work. The atmosphere is nice but the work is really tiring and very noisy. I'm so exhausted I almost fainted twice in one month. I'm preparing my departure for Belfast; as usual, I will make a stop in Dublin to visit Noémie and Pauline. I call my manager at Wellington College but she doesn't seem as friendly as Tiffany.

My sister and brother-in-law come back from their holidays during daytime. When I arrive home in the evening that same day, it is to find a few things I had, according to them, left lying around in the kitchen, in a jumble. My brother-in-law is compulsively obsessed with order. During my stay, I had baked cakes and cooked homemade dishes that I had frozen to thank them for their hospitality, but my sister bluntly tells me that they will not touch them because they do not like what I cook!

It's time to go back to Ireland and so I don’t linger.

Part II

Belfast, end of August 1990

I make my way to Belfast on my own because no one is waiting for me. My manager has booked a room for me on campus at Queen's University. I still have to find accommodation, as I don't have any. I browse through all the classifieds until Dominique, whom I had met in Ballymena a few months earlier, contacts me. The girlfriend of her previous owner lives in Belfast and is renting a room, but she has a German shepherd and Dominique is afraid of the dog. Fortunately, I am not afraid of dogs and I take the room. So I will only stay 3 nights on campus.

I take possession of my new residence; the owner's name is Lorna. She is four years older than me. She is a nurse and currently training as a midwife. At first sight, she seems cold but she, in fact, has a lot of humour. She is a brunette, quite tall; she has white skin and a slight squint.

She recently moved into a new single-storey building at the end of a lane of semi-detached apartments. My room overlooks a small courtyard. The bedroom is fully furnished with recycled goods. The mattress is patched up with thick tape to prevent the springs from going any further! There is a small sofa on the side, a small wardrobe but no shelves or chest of drawers. I'll make a sort of cardboard trunk that I'll cover with wallpaper.

So this year I will be living near the Belfast city centre, in a quiet Protestant neighbourhood on the edge of the Ormeau Park. I will have a twenty-minute walk to go to Wellington College, crossing this beautiful green space, where there is a large golf course. Every day, I will look out over the mountains, and it will bring me joy. Rather, as the Irish say, the mountain will wish me a good day.

After over a month, I call my parents. My father tells me that he is about to wire ten thousand Francs (£1300) into my account, following Grandma's inheritance. This is the first time my father has ever given me money. He never cared, neither for me nor for my sisters. I think he felt a break between us two, when we used to be so tight before. He's trying to fix something, to show he's thinking of me. I thank him very much. I'm thinking about buying a car to get around whenever I feel like it. Now I will have the means. In the meantime, I buy a second-hand bike.

Wellington College

Walking to school is more of a stroll in this pleasant park. Wellington College is huge next to the establishments I attended in Antrim. It is, in fact, two establishments that have merged. Until last year, there were two French assistants; but this year, for budgetary reasons, there is only one and that's me. So they add three hours of paid overtime, which is a good surprise. I'll be able to save some money.

I meet the head of the French department, my manager, Miss G. Her French is very good, just as Mr Wilson's in Antrim was. This person seems to come out of a comic book caricature. She looks like Bette Midler. A very plump woman, wearing too short dresses, very exuberant and endowed with an incredible authority. She has a very bad reputation but she is an excellent teacher. I even discovered Françoise Sagan thanks to her. I studied "Bonjour tristesse" (Hello sadness) with her students. She could have taught a literature class like a true Frenchwoman. As she had been in this school for over 20 years, she had some kind of "power" and no one could manage to drive her out. What a strange persona. Many a teacher has existed in her shadow, including me.

I also meet other French teachers, Mr Bingham and Mr Thompson, and then a geopolitics teacher, Mr Smylie. To this day, we keep in touch. Aaron Smylie is somewhat aside in this establishment. Physically, he reminds me of Lenin, and I'm not far from it since he publicly displays his socialist sensibility and his atheism! This is exactly what it takes, in Northern Ireland, to be marginal. His personality stands out and, very quickly, we will become friends and, with good reason, as I am constantly questioned about my faith. I always answer that I am Catholic since baptism but non-practicing and atheist. It seems difficult to understand because in Ireland you are either Catholic or Protestant. So some students are even asking me if I am "Catholic atheist" or "Protestant atheist"; a famous joke in Ireland says that when you are a Catholic atheist or a Protestant atheist, you are necessarily... Jewish!

For the Northern Irish, I am stateless because religion is their identity. To be Catholic is to be pro-Republican and to be Protestant is to be pro-British. The choice is singularly limited.

I have often been invited to masses or "services" in one church or the other, this intrigues me a lot. People just don't understand that I don't have a "side".

In September, the German assistant - whose name I do not remember - also arrives. She will only stay for a month. She will be replaced by Conny who will be the first East German graduate from the University of Jena to come to a "Western" country after the fall of the Berlin Wall.

I foresee this year with less enthusiasm than the previous year. Moreover, the events of the summer with my mother and father, weigh on me like a heavy burden. And then, still no man in my life. I am 24 years old and nothing is happening. Maybe I am not normal; I even wonder if I'm a lesbian. However, I'm not attracted to any woman in particular despite the large number of girl friends around me!

***

One October morning, a young blonde woman arrives, she's a little lost at Wellington College. Miss G. introduces her to me. She's the new German assistant. She comes from Jena and has never been to an English speaking country before. She is very tall, skinny, with slightly droopy blue eyes, and curly hair. She lives on campus.

After visiting the establishment and seeing her schedule, I suggest that she comes to my place where I can help her to settle in. The next day, I even offer her to move into my room while she's looking for an accommodation. I am so spontaneous that I forget I am not at home and Lorna, my landlady, points it out to me! I tell her that I will pay her extra and that it is only temporary. Anyway, Conny is already here, she doesn't really have a choice. Eventually, all is going well. Conny is friendly and helpful and Lorna is looking after her as well. We can tell that she is lost in both this western world and this country at war. Her eyes are wide open when she sees police stations, armoured vehicles and household appliances that she has never seen in East Germany. Lorna's friend, John, lends her a bicycle to go to work at another school, as she has to go to the northern part of Belfast, to St Malachy, a Catholic school.

Moving to Northern Ireland is a culture shock for her.

From this unique encounter a true great friendship is born between us. I will be her maid of honour nine years later and she will be mine in 2004. "Conny" will be my daughter's middle name.

***

This year, as I am close to the university, I decide to take the Proficiency Certificate of English at Queen's University Belfast. I had already started classes when I was an au pair, in the suburbs of London, but I had stopped everything to return to France after six weeks. This was four years ago. This diploma certifies a level of English close to that of a person whose mother tongue is English. It is recognised worldwide in universities and companies. Conny and I apply and get to know other students including a couple from Hungary.

When I saw Klapisch's movie "L'auberge Espagnole" (Pot Luck), I myself felt like I was living in this carefree student atmosphere, which I had never experienced before as I started working very early. I never really "mingled" with others.

Our teacher is actually a linguistics teacher and this catches my attention. He studies and analyses the different accents of Ireland and I find this captivating. I am the only one of this group of about forty young people who pays attention to his work. He gives me part of his lessons and a tape of the different accents recorded in Ireland. He has another one with Belfast accents. It's fascinating.

It is also in this group that I meet Pere, a Spaniard. He is my age exactly; we are just one day apart. Our wee fling will not begin until April and it is only October!

With other students from all over, we will take beautiful walks, rhymed by our different accents, which make purebred Irish turn around in the Botanical Gardens. This is very fun. It adds colour to this unique green that makes Ireland!

***

Just like the previous year, the Wellington College music teacher suggested that I audition to enter the Belfast Philharmonic Choir. I only have "Molly Malone" to audition. He's prepping me for it. I get a time at the end of the day to audition. What a surprise when I discover that I am not alone and that the candidates are all musicians with a thick score in their hands! I simply arrive with a tiny score folded in half, stored in my purse. I'm convinced it is not going to work out. When it's my turn, I enter a large room where the piano seems tiny. I give Molly Malone's sheet music to the pianist. The conductor tells me to start. I sing four or five bars and then I am given scales to follow. It lasts a total of maybe five or ten minutes tops. They bid me farewell. I'm thinking I was right; it's over. Coming downstairs, a woman gives me a paper to fill out and gives me a time the following evening to rehearse. I don't understand and ask her if I was selected or not. She answers positively! I cannot believe it. I am a member of the Belfast Philharmonic Choir and our rehearsals will take place at the

Ulster Hall!

Conny, who is a musician, will also join me in the choir.

From All Saints' Day to the Christmas holidays, most of my outings will be with Conny and Dominique, who brought her car back from France. We go to Catholic pubs to hear traditional music. Dominique has a habit of drinking a Guinness or two and smoking weed at the same time. This puts her in a hallucinogenic state, which makes her very funny. We know she's going to come out of the pub and then go around it twice, running and laughing out loud. Then we go to the opposite potato shop to eat a big stuffed potato that will soak up the alcohol. I, myself, don't drink alcohol except for an occasional glass of cider

End of December 1990

Conny and I respectively go back to Germany and France. A new accommodation will be waiting for Conny in January. She will come back later than I will.

I'm taking the plane; Valérie is expecting me, as usual. I'm visiting my friends, maybe my sister, I don't quite remember.

I am going to visit my parents; they even wrote to me during this term. My mother sent me cooking recipes!

There, I am shocked. My mother is not the same anymore. My father takes care of her like he would of a little girl. He flatters her, tells her that she has mastered her mayonnaise, that it's good. When I arrived, they were preparing a "cassoulet" but I could tell that my father was the one doing everything, even though he wants me to believe otherwise. She hardly speaks any more, her face has changed, her body too. She places her fingers on her temples. She must have a bad headache. She is weak.

When she is moving she's crawling against the wall, it's impressive. Her legs are no more than sticks; she doesn't have any more muscles. Her belly is huge.

She's a wreck. Yes, I have to face the facts: I have, in front of me, a woman who has been drinking alcohol for at least thirty years, combining strong analgesics, or other drugs, as long as it puts her in the most hallucinatory state possible. It's terrible. She is my mother. The one I only call mom under duress. But she's not a mother. She's a drunk. A wasted being that is about to fall. A being that is acting addictive and self-destructive. She disgusts me.

I have a bad feeling and I share it with my father before I leave. He tells me that everything is fine!

I also learn that John causes disciplinary problems, even of delinquency. I try to talk to him. I feel sorry with this state of play. And I'm powerless.

I'm leaving from Le Havre where I'm taking the ferry. My aunt Janine is bringing me there. She has bronchitis and often stops. My uncle no longer drives. He has Alzheimer's disease but we do not yet officially know.

As I arrive in Le Havre, there is a very strong storm. The ferry will take 24 hours to get to Rosslare instead of 16 hours. A hell of a journey!

In Rosslare, I tell Noémie I'm stopping by to see her in Bray. She tells me that she is expecting a baby.

I take the express back to Belfast; I will arrive around 5 p.m. at Lorna's. Nobody is there. I'm alone. I'm exhausted and can't think anymore.

Lorna and John come home. They are here to get dressed as they are going to celebrate the New Year with friends. I greet them and tell them I'm going to bed. They leave.

I find myself alone in my cold room. I start to cry. I go and get all the medicines that I have in my possession and put them on the box that stands as my bedside table. I cannot stand it anymore. I want to die. I'm tired of being alone. No one is attracted to me. I go and get something to eat to swallow them all. I come back to the room. I'm looking at those pills. Yes, I'm going to ditch myself, like my sister.

And then I hear the front door open. It's Lorna and John! Wow ! They call me in case I am not sleeping yet. They tell me that finally they are celebrating New Year's at home and that a couple of friends are coming over. I don't really know where I am anymore. I hide the tablets, I don't even remember where. I reflect on what I just did!

So I come into the living room. John and Lorna have opened a bottle of port and, with their friends, we have a drink at midnight. Then, as I'm so exhausted, I just go to bed, for good! I eventually wake up thirteen hours later in the middle of the afternoon.

I then realised what I had done the day before and thought to myself that I would have put Lorna in significant trouble. This failed attempt directed me to research on suicide. A year later when I will be in Coutances in Normandy, I will understand that I was a "victim" of the "daughter of an alcoholic mother" pattern. Learning this (by myself, without a shrink) has helped me enormously to move forward, towards life.

It's January 1st, 1991; a new year is beginning!

***

Conny comes back from Germany with lots of gifts and cooking utensils to make Thüringe specialties. She will soon be moving to her new home.

Since I have enough savings to buy a used car, I go through all the classifieds. We have agreed with Conny to share the costs of insurance and fuel for the next six months. We know that we'll both have visitors and it will be convenient to be able to drive everyone.

I find an option in a garage not far from my home. I call Mark, then my father, to find out what I should "put to test" so I don't get fooled. So I know that if I can start in second, the clutch is defective. I test the brakes. I look at the tires. I am not an expert on the subject. I see that the car has been repainted but I do not see that it has also previously burnt! The only thing that bothers me is the seat belt: I can't get it fastened because my seat is so far forward it doesn't buckle. The mechanic laughs pretty loudly and says: "It's not the belt that's too small, it's you!" And that's true. I am very petite for a woman in Ireland. To buy shoes, I have to go to the children's section and can only find sports shoes!

I buy this car, a red Ford Fiesta. I am pretty amazed as I am not afraid to drive on the other side of the road and of the car. I have no problem with the opposite gear pattern. I'm very proud of myself after all.

I go home and park the car in front of the apartment, in the courtyard. Lorna comes home from work shortly after, parks next to the Fiesta. She is flabbergasted because she went to see a psychic, as she often does, and she just told her that she would have a red car next to hers in the coming days! She adds that this psychic is truly very good.

Conny also arrives at home. She goes and checks out the car, our precious! As I am curious, I ask Lorna for the contact details of this famous psychic. Her home is not accessible by transport; luckily, now that I have a car, I'll be able to go. Conny is also very interested and we quickly make an appointment with this woman who lives in Bangor. We will not see her until three weeks later, just after my friend Gaëlle's visit - she is a pharmacist whom I met in Dublin in 1987.

Gaëlle arrives at the end of January, around her birthday. She will be staying for a week. She brings me the latest ointment released for psoriasis and massage oils. She is delighted to visit Belfast and meet Conny. She will then host her in Paris for several years. Conny's friend from London also shows up, unannounced. I don't recall where he stayed but I do remember that he got along pretty well with Gaëlle! We went to the Giant's Causeway, a real madness at this time of the year, but it was fun. I only remember the pouring rain, the strong wind and those dark clouds above us.

Gaëlle insists on taking a picture of Conny and I in front of our beautiful car, which she calls Elco, for Elsa and Conny! To this day, this story has stuck with the both of us.

***

One afternoon, we eventually meet this so-called extraordinary woman, the palm reader from Bangor. Her house is ordinary and so is she! She seems calm. She oozes some kind of wisdom. She tells us what she does, how she proceeds. A true pedagogue!

She reads hands' lines and then reads in tea leaves. This is not common.

She's a woman who wants to help, who wants to communicate, and send messages; it's palpable. She has the patience of a saint. She is explaining to us how we should apply lipstick on the inside of the hand. She is showing us how lines stand out and what they mean. She is genuinely sharing her "knowledge": she discloses how you recognise a boy from a girl when you are expecting, separations, and the number of significant encounters!

This woman is fascinating.

Regarding me, she is telling me that I will not be a frequent traveller, that my life is not in Ireland (I don't believe it!), and that I will teach all my life (she does not know that I teach). She is also telling me that my voice will be very important to me and that it will be useful in my life. She then goes on and adds that I often get lost in unnecessary details and that it will harm me. She tells me that I will have three pregnancies and two children, first a girl and then a boy. They will study for much longer than I did.

The man of my life is not for now, she tells me, I will have to be patient, and wait! He will be a musician, three or four years older than me.

Then comes the tea leaves reading. She makes me pour a cup of tea, with the leaves, on a white plate. She shows me the convolutions and the paths that my future life will make me take. I understand everything; it speaks to me. She talks to me about my mother even though I haven't even mentioned her. She tells me that her eyes are hurting, that she's going blind - my mother just told me on the phone that she couldn't see anymore. She adds that she will go into hospital and never leave. On the day of her funeral, I shall receive a blue letter for a job offer. I will make two round trips to France, including a boat trip. At my current job, a woman who is jealous of me will betray me. I will even lose my job.

I see her eating dried fruit, a bit like a smoker who chews gum so as not to smoke, and why - I don't know - I ask her if she is an alcoholic. She replies that she was, that she is now a "dried alcoholic" therefore abstinent but that, deep down, she is.

As for Conny, she tells her she will get married, have two professional careers, one in teaching and the other in publishing or journalism. She will have one child. She will divorce and a very long friendship is beginning between us.

At the end of the consultation, I hand her money. She takes the banknote, gives it back to me and says: "Take it, I hope I am wrong". I try in vain to give it back; she does not want it and says: “good luck". I guess she has the news of my mother's future passing in mind.

Conny and I look at each other without saying a word. She

accepts Conny's banknote.

I thank this very unique woman. I'll never forget her, neither will Conny. I am disturbed by her "clairvoyance", her mediumship, and her humanity. She's the kind of person you only meet once in a lifetime. She was not a fraud. I could feel it. The future will prove the accuracy of almost all of her statements.

As I plan to move to Northern Ireland, I am looking for part-time jobs that will pay for fuel for the car and keep me from spending my salary. I reply to an ad a blind woman posted, she's looking for a housekeeper. I will work for this person for several weeks. Then I apply at a supermarket where I first get a job as a cashier, and then as an ice cream seller in the shopping arcade. I work there for a few hours on Fridays, when I'm off. I'm trying to set my mark all over the place to show that I can adapt to all kinds of jobs.

One day, I even answer to an official posting at the Belfast employment agency. It's for a home seller job for Miko ice creams. I get a meeting very quickly in their rather impressive premises. I'm interviewing with a man and a woman who ask me a lot of questions, and with whom I feel very comfortable. I already know I won't get the job but the interview was a real treat. I think they were curious as to why a 24-year-old French woman was applying for this kind of job and I'm sure they had as good a time as I did. The woman tells me I can return whenever I want; chatting with a French woman must be pleasant, it's exotic and French people don't exactly grow on trees in Belfast!

With Florence, another French assistant, we are going to the St Patrick procession which takes place every year on March 17th, in Downpatrick, the city where the Saint had settled in Ireland. It's raining and it's cold. We were only supposed to be spectators but we end up taking part in the procession and climbing the hill with everyone to reach the top. We are happy to have done it and even feel a certain pride and serenity, despite the incessant rain.

My friend Nathalie is visiting and this time I intend to tour part of Ireland by car. I'm picking her up at the bus station. As she is getting off the bus, I see Pere next to her; he is one of the students with whom I am preparing the Proficiency Certificate. Our eyes meet and something happens between us. I ask him if he is getting home by bus and offer to drive him back. He accepts.

I drop Pere off, in front of his house; he thanks me and gives me his phone number. I don't remember if I gave him mine!

Nathalie, just like last year, tells me that I have changed. She senses I'm comfortable, at ease, with myself. And I see her happy to be here in Ireland, visiting this beautiful country.

Thanks to my story telling about the palm reader, Nathalie had asked me to book an appointment for her. She is just as fascinated by this unique character as we were. She is describing her job to her: "you are close to bodies, you see them but you do not touch them" - Nathalie was a radiology technician. She's telling her about her marriage, an only child, a divorce and a moment on a lake (she will go to Quebec and make an excursion on a great lake).

With Nathalie, we have been driving for a fair amount of miles and luckily the weather is very nice. I'm hoping the car doesn't break down, and it actually holds up. I am not afraid. I have confidence. If anything happens, there will always be someone to help me; I know it even if I don't know whom. There is always someone, for sure.

We are passing through very rolling landscapes but almost desolate and desert, it is an unusual landscape for us French. Nathalie is taking pictures. She is amazed. We are heading to Londonderry, London for Protestants (the British) or Derry for Catholics and Anglicans. We notice that two cathedrals face each other. One is Catholic, Saint Eugene, which was built following the Catholic Emancipation Act of 1829. The other is Anglican, Church of Ireland (close to the Catholic religion); it is Saint Colomba, older and dating from the 17th century. It's amazing for us French to have two cathedrals in one city. Nathalie, who is a believer and practicing, does not understand this split either. It was in this city that the "Troubles" began with the famous "Bloody Sunday", the day when fourteen Catholics were shot dead by the English Army during a pacifist march. That city does not have a good reputation. Arriving in front of the guesthouse, I lock the car doors and close them, but not without leaving my keys inside! I ask the first passer-by I see if he could help us. A fairly chubby man helps us out by going to look for a neighbour who arrives with a thick wire that he adapts during his intervention. He forces the window and inserts the wire, which he previously hooked, to reach the latch. He is successful. I warmly thank him and collect the luggage we need.

Everything seems so simple.

I booked a guestroom which appears majestic to us: the old bathroom includes a bathtub with well polished copper taps, the bedroom is beautifully decorated, the owner could not have been nicer, and breakfast is hearty and delicious.

We go on, while the sun and landscapes keep us company. We are heading towards Enniskillen on the shores of Lough Erne. The town is flat and almost deserted, that's the impression it gives us. It has been the stronghold of the Loyalists since the Crown colonised it in the 17th century. The city was the scene of violence linked to the "Troubles" in support of IRA hunger striker Bobby Sands. Eleven people were killed there on November 7, 1981.

We are observing the rather imposing 16th century castle. The weather is changing for the worse and the lake is taking on a grey colour.

We continue to Belleek, the porcelain town competing with Donegal's porcelain, just across the border. It's the same land but not the same nation.

Landscapes seem strange; like desolate, poor, and abstract!

While we are driving, Nathalie and I talk very little, as if the environment took up all the space.

Our wee three-day getaway is now coming to an end so we head back to Belfast.

We will both keep a unique, secret, memory of this journey.

Nathalie returns to Paris, her head full of images.

May 1991

Conny's father comes to visit his daughter. Since the German reunification, he has lost his job as a mechanical engineer and will never work again. He, therefore, has time on his hands. He is a very discreet man, truly kind, and who shows empathy. We'll go out once together.

I ring Pa Pi Ja more often. The news is not good. My mother can't see anything anymore; she can't get up from her bed. My dad says she's not making any effort to get better.

In the meantime, I'm invited to a party at Pere's. He shares an apartment with four other students, including two apprentice chefs from Italy. There are two very kind young women.

Pere is handling the making of a Spanish omelette, a "tortilla". He is preparing it in front of me and, as he is looking at me, he throws the egg in the bin whilst keeping the shells in his hand! It's funny and we laugh! Life is beautiful!

Later in the evening, I would even say in the wee hours, Pere offers me to sleep at their place. He asks one of his roommates to let me use her room. I first refuse but they all insist. My car has broken down, it wouldn't start, I am on foot, and I do not live close by. I finally accept.

The young woman lends me a nightgown. It is chilly and humid in the house. I eventually go to bed but half an hour later, Pere knocks on the door, opens it and asks me if he can sleep with me. I do not really know what to answer but I ultimately agree.

He hops into bed and gets close to me. He bursts out laughing when he sees my ladybug socks. He asks me why I'm wearing socks at night. He doesn't know I'm cold. I am cold 24/7. Not much happens because Pere falls asleep quickly, and then, I leave very early in the morning to call my parents.

Not much happened but enough to leave me unsettled!

Pere calls me back in the morning to tell me that I didn't say goodbye to him when I left.

I'm living this wee fling intensely; I both cling to it and detach myself from it. I'm afraid of hurting, of suffering from this relationship that is so inconsistent.

One morning, I call my parents and my mother hardly tells me anything. I ask her if she wants me to come back and, at once, she answers: "no, stay where you are, you are fine there". Surprised by this unexpected response, I tell her that I'm coming to see her. I hang up and start crying, without even realising it. I inform the school that I have to leave to visit my mother who is ill. I also notify the supermarket.

I drive downtown to book a flight for the next day. I park the car in a "control zone", but don't even pay attention to it. I manage to find a flight for the next day, with a stopover in Manchester.

As I'm coming back to my car, I can see from afar a traffic ticket on my windshield. I've never had one before. I'm angry but, never mind, that's the way it is. Murphy's law in full effect: if something can go wrong, it will !

Conny prepares a salad from her native Thüringe for me because she noticed that I hadn't been eating much lately.

The next day, Conny drives me to Belfast Airport. I'm leaving for France, compelled by the situation.

At the stopover in Manchester, I get thoroughly controlled and my salad, which reeks of garlic, is confiscated. It is true that I could have hidden a bomb inside; I obviously look like a terrorist! I'm trying to explain this to the customs officers - who are doing their job but are prodigiously annoying me at this precise moment! They are not making me laugh! I have so much more to think about.

Regnéville-Coutances

Once I arrive in Paris, I call Pa Pi Ja and my father tells me that my mother has been rushed to the hospital, which I expected. I tell myself that, at least, I'll see her before she leaves forever!

I take the subway and then head to the Saint-Lazare train station. Ticket in hand, I board the train, the train that will take three never-ending hours to reach its destination. Time is both long and empty.

Once I arrive in Coutances, my father takes me directly to the hospital. He bought me an almond croissant, which he carefully stored in the glove compartment. He knows I love them.

My mother was hospitalised on a Saturday. My sister, whose in-laws live in Calvados, thirty miles from Regnéville, came by and helped her eat yogurt. My mother can no longer feed herself.

When I enter the room, I discover a woman whose face has completely changed. Her face goes into spasm. As I'm getting closer, she's smiling at me. I think she recognises me but in fact she's calling me "Mammy" and never stops telling me "Mammy, Mammy, Mammy !" My father is tenderly caressing her, kissing her all over the face, while she's pushing him away, refusing his gentle strokes, and she keeps saying to him: "bastard, bastard!" but he perseveres, he disregards everything around him, as if he was consoling a crying baby.

She is offered to drink some coloured water supposed to fake the colour of wine, but she tastes it and spits it out right away, saying it's disgusting!

I know it is the end, even though I haven't seen the surgeon who's treating her yet. Her belly is huge compared to her skeletal limbs. I ask the staff why and I am told it is ascites, a fluid that is secreted by the liver when it is sick. The liquid has been drained but it’s building up again.

Upon returning to Pa Pi Ja, my father insists that I sleep next to him. I dare not refuse for the first night but the next day I go to see my aunt Janine and ask her for hospitality.

My mother's bed is shockingly filthy, full of blood and dried stool. It disgusts me.

As I had planned, I will go see my aunt Janine the next day. She does not know that my mother is hospitalised because they are angry at each other, since the Pa Pi Ja inheritance. I inform her that my mother is about to die and ask her if she, and my uncle Alfred, are willing to come over at Pa Pi Ja for a drink.

Janine feels sorry, it shows, she is distraught. She paces the room, then comes back to me and says: "Elsa, I have a chicken in the freezer. I'll cook my onion chicken. Come and have lunch tomorrow".

I am so relieved. The wall collapsed on its own, so did hate and jealousy.

I ask if I can stay over and, of course, she accepts.

The next day, the reunion is very moving. My father has tears in his eyes as he walks through the gate to their front garden. This gate that remained closed for so long. Janine invites him in. They both are very touched, my uncle as well. They do not hug each other, because we don't do that, but the emotion is palpable.

I now know that I will be able to return to Belfast in peace. Janine will take care of everything when the time comes. I don't have to worry anymore. My father will not be alone.

During my short stay in Regnéville, I see my father living in a dream, utter nonsense. He leaves several times a day to look for the necessary material to redo the living room tapestry, which is faded. He wants the house to be nice and clean when my mother comes back home! He keeps going and does not even ask the surgeon for any information. That same surgeon who is telling me that she will not make it or rather if she comes out she will "feet first", those were his actual words.

I'm changing my plans. I'm telling myself that I will not be able to stay in Ireland while leaving my father and John alone. It is just not possible; and actually without my mother, it will be easier, I will be free.

I book my trip on the ferry leaving from Cherbourg. It is the most practical and, above all, least expensive. My father drives me there, and ends up crying in my arms, squeezing both my hands tightly. It's not customary for him but the situation is unprecedented.

Belfast end of May

The boat ride is long and I start writing. I am putting together a chronological plan to write about my life, which is only twenty years long. I put words on the diary Nathalie gave me nine years ago. I always have it with me. I'm designing, then erasing, and then redoing the plan. I have no explanation for this sudden urge to write my life, then and there, it's stronger than me. I have to make this plan to be able to write. I did not book a cabin and am sleeping in the common room. Around three in the morning, the on duty staff is hoovering, which wakes me up.

In Dublin, my friend Noémie is waiting for me at the Busaras bus station to say hello, before I take the bus back to Belfast. She will soon give birth.

Back in Belfast, Conny is picking me up by car. She lets me know that the exhaust pipe broke and that it had to be replaced. In a few days, I have to take two exams for the Proficiency Certificate. I haven't been able to study.

I tell Conny about my plan to go back to France and live there.

I see Pere two or three times. I don't sense that he is in love but he wants to come to France, maybe even live there for a few months and so I start building up high hopes. I'm telling myself that he does care. I want to believe it.

One day when I call him at home, I learn that he is in the hospital for appendicitis. I rush to the Royal Hospital. I run to the reception desk to ask in which wing he is hospitalised. At last, I find his unit and expect, as in France, to walk a long corridor leading to private rooms, but I do not see any. They are, in fact, large rooms where beds are separated by a curtain. It reminds me of war action movies. I find Pere's bed and to my great surprise, I see a young woman at his bedside holding his hand! Pere sees me and greets me. He seems very tired and I find myself standing there like a fool, at the bedside of someone who's clearly played me. I am disappointed and sad.

I resume teaching in high school. Miss G, my manager in charge of the French department, invites me to the restaurant for the first time in the year. She had recently offered, despite the circumstances, to extend my contract by one month. I would prep students for their French A Levels. I would also supervise exams. I had accepted her offer. I would keep this job until the end of June. I eventually understand, during lunch, that this proposal no longer holds. She tells me that the next day will be my "presentation day". At first, I don't know what that means. But I quickly understand. "Presentation Day" means the "day of the presentation of gifts", with the accompanying thanks. So my contract does end at the end of May, as originally planned. The financial consequences worry me because of the last and upcoming trips to France that were not planned.

One day, coming home from school, I feel bad, on the verge of fainting. I stop walking as my belly hurts a lot. I can feel a flow between my legs. Fortunately, I am not far from the Medical Centre, so I walk there, doubled over with pain. A gynaecologist examines me. He tells me that I just had a miscarriage. Truthfully, I haven't been taking my pill the way I should have.

Strangely, this episode does not rattle me. It does not make me sad. I'm leaving with a treatment to "get rid of the rest", as the gynaecologist puts it. This event just piles up with everything else, without a dramatic result. Now is not the time!

Years have passed. I wanted to believe in this fling with Pere, and show that, at 25, I could have someone in my life. Twenty-five was a symbolic age in the sewing world. My mother was a trained seamstress and she insisted, heavily, familiarly, on this point. If you were single at 25, you would remain an old spinster. I didn't want that. So I had a physical relationship a few days before I turned 25. The miscarriage probably "formalised" this event in my existence.

On November 25th of that same year, my aunt Janine placed the dreaded Saint-Catherine hat[1] on my head. I was indeed single. I was sad despite the party. She even wrote a card that said:

---

[1] Tradition when a woman remains unattached at the age of 25

"How about a little husband?" It was custom, tradition. It was foolish.

I'm feeling extremely tired, drained, that's what I remember the most. My heart beats fast every single day. I know the phone will soon ring and I'll hear the dreaded news.

I take my written exams for my Proficiency Certificate. Then I'll have one final oral test on June 11.

A few teachers invite Conny and me to the restaurant. Aaron introduces me to his family, and his home in Lisburn. I'm enjoying these last moments.

June 8th

Conny notices I have gotten much thinner and decides to come and sleep, with me, in my room, to watch over me. She is worried. She can tell I'm different, disconnected. She is angry at Pere.

At 7 a.m., the phone rings. I rush to the phone. It's Janine. "You know why I'm calling you. She passed a bit earlier!" Lorna comes out of her room and gets it right away. Janine is sharing the news very calmly and with great tenderness. It's June 8th. I'm starting to cry like never before. I don't know what it is to cry, I never cry.

I go to the travel agency and book a ticket for the next available flight. Conny comes along. Lorna pulls out a huge empty travel bag and tells me to start packing all my things, whatever I can take now. I do not want to. I don't want to leave for good. Still, I know she's right.

After booking and packing, I head to the living room and curl up in a chair, in a foetal position. Conny and Lorna are trying to force me to do something else but I can't.

My aunt calls me back to tell me that the funeral will take place on June 11th. It's the day of the Proficiency oral test.

My friends offer to come and pick me up at the airport but for once my sister rings and asks if, by any chance, it would suit me if they came to pick me up at the Charles de Gaulle Airport. She also tells me how happy she is: her company's policy allows her to have three days off thanks to our mother's funeral! I accept. We will leave together, by car, for Regnéville.

The following night, I didn't sleep. I spoke German through most of the night to poor Conny who had to bear with me. My German had never been so good, apparently!

June 9th, Ezanville

My sister Chantal and her husband Denis come to pick me up at the airport. They are rather smiling as if nothing had happened. We leave for Ezanville, where they live. Their bathroom is under construction. A shower has been temporarily installed in the basement of their house, on the cement, but despite everything my brother-in-law explains that I must not wet the cement around the shower. I imagine this is of the utmost importance when you are about to go to a funeral!

June 10th, Regnéville

We arrive in Regnéville in the afternoon, after having lunch with Denis' parents. They salute my father, drop me off and go back to the in-laws to return the next day, the day of the funeral.

My father is a mere shadow of himself. He no longer knows what to do. He asks me to go to the marble factory to choose the tomb. I pick pink Balmoral. It’s clear and bright. It reminds me of Ireland, it's the name of a town in Northern Ireland.

In fact, I'm taking over for my aunt, Janine.

In turn, the next day, she tells me that her husband, Alfred, has Alzheimer's disease. I do not know this pathology. She tells me it's precocious senility. Alfred is only 63 years old.

More bad news on top of the others!

June 11th

Chantal and Denis join us at Pa Pi Ja. John, my nephew, is present as well.

My father asks us what we are going to tell people if they ask us what our mother died of. While I disagree, they still decide to say that she died of liver cancer. It sounds better to say that than the actual truth.

Just before leaving, my father lets me know I have a letter in the drawer of the telephone cupboard. The letter has been sitting there for a few days but, considering the events, he forgot to tell me about it. It's a blue letter! Wow, this can't be! The palm reader had told me about this. I'm getting chills everywhere. I open the letter: it's from the Caen Board of Education. This is a job offer for an English replacement job at a Secondary School. I no longer remember that I had contacted the Board of Education and applied for a job. It's been months, maybe a year, or even more!

The replacement work is scheduled to begin on this day, June 11th. This is obviously not possible. I will call the Board of Education when I come back from the funeral.

Denis, proud of his young sister-in-law, says to me: "you, you'd find water in the desert!"

Mass has been scheduled at the Grimouville Church. We are all waiting in front of the church. My aunt Pierrette - my mother and Janine's sister - as well as my uncle Michel, dressed in a tailcoat for the occasion, come to me. They ask me, in a rather aggressive tone, why I did not come and say hello to them. Meanwhile, local neighbours kindly come to see us.

Mass was never-ending and of the utmost hypocrisy. I hate funeral masses, full of lies, a performance for everyone. I'm mad.

The burial takes place at the Regnéville cemetery. It's windy on this little hill, but I have a feeling, I don't know why, that my mother will be well here and at peace.

Since that day, when I feel like it, I go to her grave and talk to her.

Once the funeral is over, we meet at Janine's who has prepared snacks. Chantal suggests leaving and says goodbye to my father. Denis, who seems surprised, and recommends staying with us for the day. Chantal accepts and says: "why not?!" The thought of staying hadn't even crossed her mind.

I call the Board of Education as soon as I get a chance and explain the situation. I am told that the position is still vacant and that they have no one to carry out this replacement job at two secondary schools. I ask them if they can wait two days for me to get organised. The Board agrees.

I definitely need a car as soon as possible and, the next day, I take care of this with Paul's friend.

If I want to be registered with the Board of Education, I must agree to whatever I am offered now, otherwise, I will not be offered anything ever again.

I barely have enough time to get a car at Robert's garage. He knows my father well, so he trusts me and agrees for me to pay monthly. My father lends me the down payment. I get my new car insured, a ten-year-old grey Polo.

I send a thank you note to all my high school teachers who supported me during this difficult time, and I mention Aaron Smylie in particular. I didn't know then what a good idea I had just had because, during my absence, an accusation was brought against him regarding me: an accusation of rape. This letter, amongst other things, will exonerate him. Miss G is the perpetrator of the complaint.

Two days after the funeral, I'm already travelling the Manche roads to do my replacement work. I really like it. The countryside is so beautiful that driving is a recreation for me. I just had one problem the first day: I found myself facing a truck on the wrong side of the road, as I had gotten used to driving in Ireland for the past six months.

This activity keeps me busy, I'm not thinking about anything apart from my students for fifteen days. I also use this time to apply for accommodation in the city of Coutances, not forgetting to mention Pere's name.

Last stay in Northern Ireland

I leave for Northern Ireland, via Dublin, where I reunite with Noémie and her baby. He was born on June 17th. A death, a birth, they say!

As soon as I arrive in Belfast, I take care of all my administrative tasks. I close my bank account. Aaron, who endlessly thanks me for the mail I sent and the testimonial I gave for him, helps me sell Elco for parts. I get 100 pounds out of it, which will pay for my return trip.

I go to the Proficiency teacher and ask him if there is a re-take exam in September but, to my regret, I learn that there is not. I'm disappointed. I have to start all over again. He tells me that my writing marks are very good and that I would have had a Grade A!

All that fuss for nothing!

I say goodbye to everyone and especially to this Ireland, with its barriers, its tanks, and its attacks. This Ireland that I will miss so much.

Epilogue

I will keep in touch with Aaron and his family, as well as with Conny and Aurora, up until this day.

Pere will send me a letter to tell me that he will not come but that he wishes me good luck and that I am "a nice girl".

I will move into a vast four-room apartment, and then, into a three-room apartment in the centre of Coutances, in la Manche. I will be a supervisor and auxiliary teacher in English for a year, for the Caen Academy. I will continue my English Bachelor at the University of Caen, via distance learning, and will finish it at the University of Villetaneuse three years later. I will move to Paris in October 1992 at the age of 26.

I will never take the Proficiency Certificate of English again.

The Proficiency Certificate is THE diploma I would have liked to obtain. In the past, my mother often made me fail exams. She even openly rejoiced at this at times. I note that she's making me fail an exam again, despite her passing.

John, after an unfinished year in "BEP d'électrotechniques" (BTEC First Diploma in Electro-technical), will join a "1ère d'adaptation" (technical Lower 6), and will then pass his "Bac Professionnel de Comptabilité" (BTEC National Diploma in Accounting).

I will show him a photograph of his mother in the summer of 1991. That is when he will see her for the first time.

I will discover a "free" Belfast, after the peace agreement in

1998, accompanied by Christophe, my future husband.

August 9th, 2015

My husband, Gwen - my eldest daughter - and I are at the Beauvais airport, more than two hours before departure, as I was unable to validate Gwen's ticket. She is due to fly to Dublin at 9:25 a.m. My friends Aaron and Eleanor are expecting her at 10:00 a.m. local time!

The teller informs us that Gwen cannot leave because she is not 16 years old! I argue that it was not specified when I booked the flight! She answers that it is written in the general terms of sales and that I should know!

I decide Gwen won't go. Then I ask the hostess if Gwen can leave if we accompany her. Her answer is, of course, positive but the round trip during the day is too expensive. The round trip over two days is more reasonable, but still too costly for us. Christophe eventually settles it and decides that I will accompany Gwen. I don't fully realise. I basically left with my purse, sandals and a light waistcoat on my back! My friends have not been informed. I fill them in by Internet, on my cell phone. Aaron doesn't understand my message. I explain to him again and I am embarrassed! He answers that it is not a big deal and that they will be happy to see me, that they will lend me clothes and that he will drive me back to the Dublin Airport tomorrow afternoon.

Christophe leaves us. He is delighted, he knows how pleased I am because he is sending me to Ireland! I, on the other hand, feel guilty, we just spent an extra €305 because I had not seen that Gwen could not travel alone before turning 16! It spoils part of this happy surprise, seeing Ireland again.

Anyway, I have no choice; I'm leaving for Dublin with Gwen. I suddenly grasp that I am taking my daughter to this country that is so dear to me! Gwen has difficulty with English because she is dyslexic. I had therefore suggested I contact Aaron and Eleanor to ask if they could find her a host family. They were willing to welcome her to their home. Aaron had called me back a week later: a former colleague, a language teacher, had found a host family for Gwen. Anna would be her pen pal and her mother Valérie would welcome her. After receiving Val and Anna Shannon's contact details, I got in touch with them. They could only accommodate her for five days because the family had planned a trip to Paris. Gwen would therefore be at the Shannon's from August 9th to 14th and then picked up by Aaron and Eleanor. I had immediately booked her round trip ticket with Ryanair.

I still remembered Aaron and Eleanor so well. She is tall and fair-haired, taller than her husband, doesn't go heavy on the make up, and has a face that exudes kindness. She always arouses warmth. She is a believer. My friendship with this couple and their children really became strong when I returned to France. They loved France. They spent their summer holidays on la Manche coast, at Barneville-Carteret, in their caravan. As I lived in Coutances, we saw each other every year. My father had become some kind of a French parent to them; in particular for Aaron who did not get along with his own father. Each year, my father would greet them when they arrived at the camp site and sometimes even in Cherbourg, where the ferry arrived. It lasted about seven years. There was something in it for everyone. My father had found children who replaced those he no longer saw.

In 1994, I brought my father to Ireland. He was flying for the first time in his life. He celebrated his 70th birthday on Irish soil. He still talks to me about it. At that time, Aaron and Eleanor's three children were still young. Eleanor had the patience of an angel with them. I admired her! They would both take their car and drive us everywhere.

I visited them again in 1998, with my niece, for Easter and with Christophe in the summer. Then, they stayed with us, on holidays, in 1999; I was pregnant with Gwen. We went there in the summer of 2002 for the last time. William, my son, was just a year old and took his first steps in Lisburn.

Settled in the plane, I speak to Gwen, describing the geographical steps, the different landscapes, that we are going to fly over. I'm in awe of my memory because I had left everything in a corner of my head and thought I had forgotten everything! In fact, I hadn't thought about this during all these years. My daughter was listening to me, but I didn't want to drown her in my memories because she was going to create ones of her own. If she found herself loving Ireland, it had to be hers and not mine! So, I kept my mouth shut. I didn't want to transfer my passion for this country, these people who were part of my history, of my past. She had to make up her own mind. I didn't want to impose my view on her; even though she knew, tacitly, implicitly, and deeply, what I thought, what I felt.

We land on time. Having only two pieces of hand luggage, we go through the corridors and customs very quickly. These past days, my foot is painful; my leg does not want to follow. Our friends are waiting for us. Eleanor first recognises us and hurries towards us, Aaron follows. What a joy to see them again! I thought my unexpected presence would disturb them, I realise that they are delighted. We greet each with kisses on the cheeks, as we do in France: they have not forgotten our habits, which are not theirs! Aaron offers us to go for a drink before setting off for Belfast. We accept. Sitting around a table, I tell them about our misadventures. Aaron, proud to have French visitors with him, takes a picture of Gwen and I, and immediately posts it on Facebook. I am embarrassed. I don't really like Facebook. But it's kind and spontaneous; it's a way to share his joy!

We leave for Lisburn where Valérie, the mother, will welcome her. I recognise Aaron's nervous hastiness, as he can't get out of the airport parking lot because of a motorist not moving in front of him. I point it out to him, to Eleanor's great pleasure as she never gets angry! There is now a motorway that goes from Dublin to Belfast and now it only takes an hour and a half to get there. It took double the time 25 years ago! Gwen falls asleep, she packed her suitcase around 1 a.m. and we left at 6.30 a.m. for Beauvais airport. I'm chatting with Eleanor as best I can. My hearing is poor and the noise of the car bothers me. I'm looking at the landscape around me. The weather is not great. I see green mountains surrounded by clouds. Ireland.

When we arrive in Lisburn, at Sprucefield car park in front of M&S, Valérie and Anna are waiting for us. We're a little late. I greet Valérie, a tall, friendly, blonde woman, and Anna, a tall, upright and shy girl. I leave Gwen in the hands of these people whom I trust. We leave each other and drive our cars our separate ways.

Here I am at my friends'. I offer them the wee gifts that I took from Gwen's suitcase: a DVD on the painters of the Oise, memories of tourists. Eleanor does some cleaning, she clears the kitchen table to make room. They weren't expecting me! These frozen images from the past are amusing. I hadn't imagined anything since I left unexpectedly. Everything had remained intact in my head. I recognise their house, almost the same decor, but, over the years, a flat screen TV, cell phones, computers, and Wi-Fi have arrived!

They added a veranda; Eleanor is surprised that I don't know it! Well, yes, they've had it for 10 years and my last visit was 13 years ago! I love verandas. I take photos.

Mark, their youngest just graduated as an EKG manipulator. He is very tall, and speaks little. He already has work. The two oldest have left the nest for several years already.

It's around 1:30 p.m. Eleanor is preparing lunch. A weekend fry up: Sausages, bacon and potato bread, followed by tea and biscuits. I'm in awe looking at my potato bread. I haven't eaten one, relished one, for at least 20 years! Eleanor is delighted; she didn't think she would make me this happy. Suddenly, I feel alive again. I am home in Ireland. I feel like I've always lived here and that I live in France out of obligation, even though it's my birth country!

Aaron, nose deep in his newspaper, says: "€300 for potato bread!" with his sharp humour. Yes, that's the price of my Beauvais-Dublin round trip (!)

After lunch, we leave for their mobile home in Cranfield, a seaside resort. Eleanor looks for warmer clothes I can borrow in her second daughter's bedroom - she still hasn't cleared her things since moving to Germany four years ago.

On the way, we stop at the small supermarket near their home. I take this opportunity to withdraw £20 because I have to take the bus tomorrow to get to the airport. Eleanor does some shopping and, knowing her, I'm sure she's going to buy some potato bread!

We are now leaving for good. The roads are narrow, full of potholes and bumps. I usually enjoy it but, today, it's terribly painful. My foot, my leg: I'm feeling throbbing pain right now. We stop at an ice cream shop. Apparently they are good and they are used to getting one on the way.

We are driving along the sea, facing the green Mourne Mountains. The water is grey. We finally arrive at the mobile home after a one-hour drive. The mobile homes are aligned. There is very little space between them, just enough to park your car. However, theirs is facing the sea and the calm that reigns is beyond words.

Eleanor turns on the kettle as soon as she walks in the small kitchen. The mobile home is pretty, a bit dated, but I like it. We are drinking a cup of tea and eating a biscuit. Eleanor then suggests that we go for a stroll on the beach. I agree with an enthusiastic yes. I put on her daughter's fleece, socks, and sneakers that are too big for me. We go for our walk; just a few steps down and we are on the beach. It's low tide, it's windy, a few rays of sun pierce through the low clouds that blanket the mountain standing in front of us. We talk just about anything that comes to mind. It's interesting. I have difficulty finding the right words, which saddens me. I'm pleased to walk in the open air. My eyes, my ears, my lungs fill up and nourish. I feel re-energised.

I’m starting to limp. We're heading back.

Later on, as we are having dinner, Aaron, a wine enthusiast and professional, opens up a bottle of red and rosé for us. He is happy to share his wine with a French woman. We are talking about current events, Muslims in Europe, general intolerance, etc.

They go for a walk. I choose to rest and check in on Gwen. I find texts from John, from my friend Nathalie who is wondering what I'm doing in Dublin, after seeing the photo Aaron posted on Facebook! I don't know what to answer; it's too long a story to tell.

Eleanor has prepared my bed with two duvets; she knows I easily feel the cold. She has brought a bunch of pillows so that I can steady myself comfortably in my bed if I am in pain. I am moved by the attention she shows, when my presence was not even expected.

I sleep badly and wake up very early. It's windy and it's raining. I wait for a reasonable hour to get up because I do not want to wake them up. I get out of bed and I'm cold. I'm brewing a cup of tea.

Eleanor gets up next. She notices that I'm cold and turns the heating on. I'm so embarrassed.

She's preparing breakfast with bacon and potato bread! Aaron also gets up.

The weather is not improving. We go out anyway to buy bread and the newspaper; I also get scones and potato bread to bring back home.

Once we are back, Eleanor shows me photos from their

Australia and New Zealand trip. They organised it themselves, away from tourist trails. The photos are magnificent and I end up dreaming of such a trip.

The weather clears up. The three of us take a walk on the beach in the sun!

Eleanor tells me that she has been coming to this beach since she was a little girl. Her parents had bought a mobile home knowing that they could not go on holidays abroad. Budget was tight. She still loves going just as much, and their children as well.

Soon, it is time to leave again. I have to take the bus in Newry to go to Dublin airport.

Again, a half-an-hour drive, which makes me suffer. My friends drop me off at the bus. I leave them and take a picture of them as they are waving goodbye. They are beautiful with their smile, so frank; I love them. I'm sad. I regret that I cannot come to Ireland more often. My English is not very good anymore.

I take the plane back to Beauvais and tell myself that, by all means, I will return to Ireland.

If Christophe hadn't insisted, I wouldn't have gone back and Gwen wouldn't have discovered Ireland that year.

All Saints' Day 2015

Valérie and Anna come to visit for four days. We are having an unforgettable time. A few days before the attacks, the Bataclan massacre.

February 2016

Christophe and I are staying in Belfast for two days. War tourism has replaced hatred and a Peace Wall has risen between Falls and Shankill. Musicians take to the streets with tin whistles, violins, and traditional music. Belfast has come back to life. Unthinkable thirty years ago.

With Aaron and Eleanor, we are having dinner at a restaurant in a neighbourhood I don't know, and which has become the heart of Belfast's cultural and night life. We are discussing the Paris attacks. Aaron points out that France is supported by the whole world, everyone is aware. They, for almost thirty years, were alone in this corner of the island, with their civil war that no one wanted to hear about. This war was raging just five hundred miles from Paris. We ignored them; we didn't care. That's a fact. Aaron is right.

The Giant's Causeway, in my opinion, has become a very expensive and spoiled tourist attraction. But at least now the site is known and recognised. The site by itself, its lunar landscape, is always worth a visit.

Summer 2016

After visiting Conny in Germany, Gwendoline returned to Anna's place in Ulster. Their bond still remains today.

It is also the year of the "yes" to Brexit.

In the referendum on 23 June 2016, Northern Ireland voted 56% in favour of keeping the UK in the EU, against the majority vote (52%) of all Britons in favour of Brexit. In this province, results were largely influenced by the issue of the border - a true powder keg of violence during the three decades of conflict.

Neither London nor Brussels want the re-establishment of a physical border on the island, this in order to preserve the Good Friday Peace Agreement, also known as the Belfast Agreement, which, in 1998, ended 30 years of bloody conflict between predominantly Protestant Unionists and Catholic Republicans, in Northern Ireland.

I watch Aaron's Facebook posts regarding a possible border, once again, between Ulster and the Republic of Ireland, which will remain a state of the European Union.

In the aftermath of the Brexit referendum, hundreds of Northern Irish people were rushing to fill in their application for an Irish passport so they could travel across Europe and not be seen as purely British. What a disappointment after so many negotiations for peace.

March 2019

My father just passed away. I send a message to Aaron. He immediately calls me. We are reminiscing about all these common memories spent with "Dayday", as he used to say. He is going to write a farewell note for the ceremony that will take place on the 2nd of April. He ends up sending me back a very long text of which I only translate a small part. It is very touching. He tells me he cried a lot and I do believe him. A tribute that comes to us from Northern Ireland. The people who are present are deeply moved.

Meanwhile, Brexit is in negotiations, the agreements are postponed from one month to the next. New incidents frequently occur at the idea of reinstating a border between the Republic of Ireland and Ulster. The United Kingdom has gone mad.

A page of history - and of my history - is turning and it throws me off.

Acknowledgements

I would like to say a "special thanks" to all the people who contributed to the writing of this book, starting with my oldest and dearest friend Nathalie who has always encouraged me, since I was 16, to write and who has always read my work with so much patience!

Thank you as well to Carole Détain who, for more than five years, has motivated me to write, advised me and regularly and assiduously read what I wrote.

Thank you to Stéphanie Watteau, who has substantially translated this novel and thank you to Marieke Veraeghe, aquarellist, in designing this cover.

Thanks to Corinne Tartare who has kindly been supporting me and reading my work for a few years now, as well as to Frédérique Sophie Braize who has never stopped believing in this story and encouraged me to publish it.

Thank you to my readers and proof-readers like Ghislaine, Loïc, Pierre Luneval, Laurence Simao and Laurence Rang.

Thanks to Caro Logan, whom I hounded during the summer, who introduced me to Nombre7 Éditions and its team.

And finally thank you to all those I may have forgotten, please forgive me if this is the case!

NomBre7 éditions

contact@nombre7.fr - 04 66 05 87 18

Imprimé en France — Février 2022

Dépôt légal premier semestre 2022